HENRY HODGKIN

THE ROAD TO PENDLE HILL

JOHN ORMEROD GREENWOOD

Pendle Hill Pamphlet 229

About the Author/John Ormerod Greenwood's unusual family name comes to him through a much loved grandfather who was a minister in the United Methodist Church. Ormerod, as he is generally known, was born in London in 1907, and began to attend Friends' Meetings after World War I because of their peace witness. He joined the Society of Friends, while a student at Cambridge, and has served it as Elder, Overseer, Preparative Meeting Clerk, and Chairman of Central Committees. He has been President of the Friends Historical Society (of Great Britain) and of the Quaker Fellowship of the Arts. In 1978 he gave the Swarthmore Lecture at London Yearly Meeting on the subject of religion and the arts under the title of "Signs of Life," and the same year completed his *Quaker Encounters,* a three volume study of Friends' international work.

His main interests have been in the theatre. He was the second President of the Cambridge University Mummers (founded by Alistair Cooke), and subsequently became organizing secretary of the Group Theatre of London which presented the plays of Eliot, Auden, Isherwood, Louis MacNeice and others with music by Benjamin Britten and settings by John Piper. For six years radio producer for the BBC, he later taught for eighteen years at the Royal Academy of Dramatic Art. His play, *The Cave and the Garden,* appeared at the Players' Theatre, London, and he wrote the libretto of an opera, *The Visitors,* with music by John Gardner, which was presented both at the Aldeburgh Festival and at Sadler's Wells Theatre in London.

Ormerod Greenwood is married, with three children and four grandchildren, and lives in Eastbourne on the south coast of England.

ISBN 0-87574-229-7

Library of Congress Catalog card number 79-91958

Printed in the United States of America by
Sowers Printing Company, Lebanon, Pennsylvania

January 1980: 2,500

COVER DESIGN by Maurine Squires, commemorating Pendle Hill's 50th Anniversary.

FOREWORD

This pamphlet embodies, in revised form, a lecture given to the Friends Historical Association and the Friends Social Union at their joint Spring Meeting at Alloway's Creek Meetinghouse, South Jersey, on Sunday May 20, 1979. Its motive was to look at the personality of the first Director of Pendle Hill, in connection with the celebration of its 50th Anniversary in 1980. Part of the research derives from my book, *Quaker Encounters:* Volume 3, "Whispers of Truth"; for this book deals with the international work of the Society of Friends in which Henry T. Hodgkin was a leading figure. This material has been supplemented from the archives of Pendle Hill, through the good offices of Eleanore Mather, and from the official biography, *Henry T. Hodgkin: A Memoir,* by H. G. Wood, published in 1937. I am grateful to Pendle Hill for the opportunity of studying the life of one of its founders during two terms' residence in 1979, in the scene he loved and helped to create. He owed much to his wife, and I owe much to mine. I am grateful also to the Friends Historical Association for permitting this paper to be published by Pendle Hill as part of the celebration of its first fifty years.

JOHN ORMEROD GREENWOOD

WHEN Pendle Hill, the Quaker Center in Pennsylvania, was founded in 1930, it was felt that much would depend on the choice of its first Director. The organizing committee decided to invite a British Friend to accept the post. Henry T. Hodgkin, then in his mid-fifties, had been one of the founders of the Student Christian Movement, had served as a missionary in China, and in 1929 was joint secretary of the National Christian Council in that country. The object of this pamphlet is to chronicle, or at least to mark the track, of his spiritual journey; to ask why a man of such wide experience was ready to accept appointment in a tiny and problematical venture (with less than twenty students at the outset); and how he, to outward appearance the complete English gentleman, became a founding father of an American institution which endured when its immediate predecessor had failed.

Quakers count the day when their founder, George Fox, climbed Pendle Hill—a high place in Lancashire where the witches held their sabbats—as a crucial day in their history. In that place of darkness Fox experienced his vision of a "great people to be gathered." Henry Hodgkin took the road to another "Pendle Hill," in the belief that everything begins in the mind and the hidden life of the soul, before it has material existence.

> Revolutions arise out of a realization of need. Given an active need and a deep realization of it, even by a few, and the revolution is already in progress. Of the awareness of this need, and of the force which it generates, we may indeed say "It builds cathedrals before the workmen have moved a stone, and it destroys them before the elements have worn down their arches. It is the architecture of the buildings of the spirit, and it is also their solvent."
>
> *(Bulletin of Pendle Hill,* February, 1932)

Henry Theodore Hodgkin was born on April 21st, 1877, in the North Country of England. He died nearly half a century ago—in that age between the wars which now seems distant history—in a Dublin nursing home on March 26th, 1933. His wife Joy, seriously ill in the same house, was carried to his room to be with him. His was a death-bed scene in the grand manner, like everything else about him. His appointment at Pendle Hill proved to be the last brief episode of a relatively short life. He had said, prophetically, "I do not know how many years I may be at this post and I want each one to count to the maximum." In that short time he set a personal stamp on the community which has endured. He established it on the basis of work, worship, recreation, and social action as "a haven of rest, a school for the prophets, a laboratory of ideas, a fellowship of co-operation." They said when he died, and surely not in mere eulogy, that "the love and devotion of Henry Hodgkin have been built into its foundation."

That is not to say, of course, that all the credit was his. Joseph Platt was the secretary of the original planning committee which invited Dr. Hodgkin to become the first director; and he and his wife Edith, reading George Fox's *Journal,* thought of the name "Pendle Hill," which was at first opposed by some of the committee ("Suppose it is in a valley?" quipped Hodgkin), but was later accepted. Behind every Hodgkin there are Platts who rarely get mentioned. Let their names, and those of many others, stand here for all the backroom dreamers.

Nor do I intend to eulogize Henry Hodgkin. But if I have later to make some remarks that appear critical, let me quote his own words in my defence. They belong to the end of his first year at Pendle Hill. The standard of his living in the beautiful house which he christened "Waysmeet" (a name now applied to another building at Pendle Hill), was apparently the subject of some comment at a Board meeting: was it consistent with the simplicity and austerity of a Quaker institution started on a shoestring? Henry was provoked to make some comment on his "employers," whose homes and ample means hardly spoke of austerity; and after the meeting Robert Yarnall wrote to soothe him. Henry replied:

> We want Pendle Hill to be the very best possible, and I am ready to submit anything I do to the judgment of my friends and fellow-workers in a way I should never dream of doing if I were merely thinking of the Board as "employers" I still feel eager to get any light I can on this whole problem, and please remember that we are learners always, and whatever helps us to see light will be welcome, whether the process be joyous or painful.

"Whatever helps us to see light will be welcome, whether the process be joyous or painful"—I hope these words give the taste of his uncompromising nobility and muscular virtue, ready to endure hard knocks with good humor—even ones received posthumously from me.

He was born among the proud Quaker clans of Darlington, "the Philadelphia of the North," as it is known in England. They had started the world's railways through their patronage of George Stephenson; they helped develop the modern steel industry and the chemical industry, their investments and contracts circled the globe, and just a few of them had built a whole new town, Middlesbrough. Their energy was matched by their intellectual range and philanthropic interests. They had been active in the anti-slavery campaign and the beginnings of Quaker "War Relief" during the Franco-Prussian War of 1870; and above all in the "Foreign Missions" which would carry the knowledge of Christ's gospel to the heathen who knew him not. In Henry's family all these things were summed up. Was not his father chairman of the Foreign Mission Association? Put the names of his parents together, and you have the clans visibly represented: Jonathan Backhouse Hodgkin and Mary Anna Pease. Of course they intermarried—would you have had them marry out?—and if they had looked further afield, where would they have found mates of comparable quality? From their genes has sprung a whole nonconformist aristocracy. Henry's uncle Thomas was the banker-historian who wrote the eight classic volumes on "Italy and her Invaders"; and his great-uncle was that Dr. Thomas Hodgkin famous in medical history (some say unfairly) for his part in identifying the painful affliction known as "Hodgkin's disease."

So Henry started with all the advantages of birth and breeding, belief and money: and solid advantages they are for creating confidence in a potential leader of men. A leader of men he certainly seemed to some who met him later. "If ever there was a perfect Prussian!" said one man after watching him chair a difficult meeting of the Fellowship of Reconciliation, "What would have happened if you had been Home Secretary?" (the minister responsible for putting the conscientious objectors in gaol.) Like all other human qualities, Henry's advantages carried with them their own built-in disadvantages against which he consciously struggled: the wish to get things settled, which lent a touch of arrogance, of knowing better; and profound ignorance of those aspects of human experience of which he had no direct knowledge: an empty belly, narrow horizons, the absence of love.

Inattentive and restless during his early years at school, in the upper forms he became notably serious and even pious. He went on to study medicine, following a family tradition, at King's College, Cambridge, and St. Thomas's Hospital in London. He was very tall (just under six feet five inches) and good at sports. He had a powerful voice and presence, and the social graces and gifts which make for ease and take the edge off awkward situations. He was famous for the parlour games he invented, often attached to mythical places; and for ghost stories. During a sea-voyage home to England from one of the preliminary discussions about Pendle Hill, he noted in a letter that he won a fountain-pen in deck games. These are the things that serious historians don't bother with, but they should, for they all create confidence and suggest a well coordinated personality. "It is good," said a sergeant-major in Hong Kong, "to get the gospel from a chap who stands over six feet in his socks."

But now we begin to note deviations from the standard pattern. Instead of any form of British football, Henry played the new Canadian game of lacrosse, and became captain of the University team at Cambridge. Instead of cricket, he played the then upstart game of lawn tennis. Bred in an English evangelical home, he can be shown to have been shaped by unsuspected transatlantic influences. The emotional tone of the period was set by those American "Revivalists" Dwight L. Moody and Ira. D. Sankey. In the student world, those were the days of the American inspired "Collegiate Christian Unions" and of the campaign to involve students in Foreign Missions. Henry's interest in these came to dominate his life. He had been caught up in the enthusiasm for missions since his boyhood in Darlington—the town which provided more men and money for the Friends Foreign Mission Association than London or any other large English city. As so often in adolescence, an indelible impression was provided by a single event: the visit to his home of the young Canadian Evangelical Friend, John T. Dorland, when Henry was eleven. Dorland spoke to an unlikely text from Judges V, 23: "Curse ye Meroz, saith the angel of the Lord, for they came not to the help of the Lord, to the help of the Lord against the mighty." Henry decided there and then that he would never be counted with the wretched inhabitants of Meroz. John T. Dorland died when Henry was 19; he brought from the New World not merely enthusiasm and charisma, but many fresh transatlantic techniques of presentation. One of his principal contributions to British Friends was to become joint secretary (with William Charles Braithwaite, future historian and son of the leading evangelical Joseph Bevan Braithwaite) of the Friends Christian Fellowship Union. This was the Quaker version of the

"Christian Unions" in the colleges; it had been founded in 1875 by a visiting American Friend, Allen Jay, otherwise known for his services to Guilford College, Greensboro, North Carolina, and to Earlham College, Richmond, Indiana. At London Yearly Meeting, Jay called the young men together and suggested that they form their own organization—for men only (women did not join until 1909) but to include attenders "with other young men as seems advisable." Revitalized by Dorland and Braithwaite, the Christian Fellowship Union soon had 900 members—including of course Henry T. Hodgkin and most of the rising leaders of the next generation of British Friends. From them would spring the "modern movement" in the Society at the end of the nineteenth century—a movement which would perhaps have hardly met with the approval of their founder, Allen Jay.

The rising power of youth had been liberated by the Romantic Movement, which had made the word "enthusiasm" fashionable, and which taught that civilization is corrupt and that we should "go back to Nature." Youth, being nearer to nature and therefore less corrupt, is superior to age, as the country is to the town, and the "noble Savage" and the peasant to the effete city-dwellers. For a long time the place of youth in the Society of Friends had been to listen to their elders until age brought wisdom and they became "seasoned Friends." Now all that was changed, and Youth began to look upon itself as a separate and enviable order in Society, close to the source of inspiration and ready to criticize its hidebound elders. In 1893 John Wilhelm Rowntree, 24 years old and speaking "as one of the youngest present," told London Yearly Meeting

> of a large and growing section who felt their thoughts out of harmony with what they heard expressed in meeting . . . if it was desired to strike home to them, they must be spoken to in their own language.

The outcome was the great "Manchester Conference" of 1895 called, as the minute says, "to dispel the ignorance in the public mind on the principles and practice of Friends; and to strengthen the attachment of its younger members to its work."

That year in Cambridge, Henry T. Hodgkin became college representative for the Christian Union there, and joined another student body of transatlantic origin, the Student Volunteer Missionary Union. This was the brain child of Robert Wilder, an American missionary who retired in 1885 from service in India to live at Princeton, New Jersey. His father had belonged to the "Brethren Club" formed at Williams College in 1806 "to effect in the person of its members a mission or missions to the heathen." Robert Wilder now revived the idea in a wider form, seeking missionary recruits among college students; he teamed up with a YMCA/YWCA team of John R. Mott and Nettie Dunn, and they invited students to take a personal pledge, "It is my purpose, if God permit, to become a foreign missionary." At a conference in 1888 the slogan of the movement, "the evangelisation of the world in this generation" first appeared in embryo form, with immediate impact. In 1892 a conference at Edinburgh, the first of the series called "Quadrennials," adopted the slogan and the name Student Volunteer Missionary Union. They issued a "Memorial" to the churches setting out their aims; this was introduced to London Yearly Meeting in 1897 by the non-Quaker J. H. Oldham, one of the future creators of the "World Council of Churches." The Clerk read the document in its entirety (it is very long) and it was printed in the *Proceedings*. Henry T. Hodgkin was a wholehearted recruit. When he applied, later on, to go to China for the Friends Foreign Mission Association, he said:

> All my life, as far as I can clearly remember, I have more or less definitely looked to this life-work. In preparing for it, I have found the blessing of God, and I look forward to it with great happiness as to the highest work possible for a man to do on earth, and I shall count it the greatest privilege to be engaged in it.

When the Student Voluntary Missionary Union found that colleges at home were scarcely less pagan than the heathen abroad (only 20 colleges in the British Isles outside Oxford and Cambridge had any sort of religious organization) they began the "Student Christian Movement," the SCM. Young Dr. Hodgkin, known to his peers by his family nickname of "Tommy," sat on its central committee, helped frame its policy, and represented it at the conference of the World Student Christian Federation at Versailles in 1900. He was made treasurer of the International Federation; and in 1901 he became chairman of the British branch of the Student Volunteer Missionary Union, an office he held until he left for China in 1905. The SVMU decided not to draw men from their denominational allegiances, but to strengthen these allegiances; and the SCM refused to be drawn into doctrinal questions, asking no more from its members than a personal pledge of loyalty to Jesus Christ. Hodgkin encouraged the practice of taking decisions without voting, and of preceding important steps by holding "retreats"—an adaptation of the Quaker process of silent waiting which he continued for the rest of his life and of which Pendle Hill is in a sense the embodiment. ("Retreats" are of course standard Catholic practice too, but not usually as an immediate prelude to executive decisions.)

Henry combined personal loyalty to Christ, derived from his evangelical background, with faith in the scientific method. His instincts were ecumenical, and he would not join either in the war of doctrine, or in the supposed war of religion and science. He was already at odds with the Fundamentalists, who refused to accept either scientific criticism of the Bible or the Darwinian theories of evolution. Some eyebrows were raised over his wholehearted adoption of the methods of "Higher Criticism" in preparing for students a Bible study book on the Epistle to the Hebrews. In 1900, when he was 23, he wrote to his friend Maxwell Lefroy, future Professor of

Entomology at Imperial College, London, a letter quoted at length in H. G. Wood's biography:

> When you say that the scientific method is to believe nothing without evidence, I emphatically agree that this should be carried into all one's life. Faith is hard to define exactly—it is certainly not believing without evidence. I should call it the active belief in a thing in which you have evidence. . . . Faith is not contrary to reason, but an act of reason. We use it constantly in science, and without it we should never advance.
>
> *Henry T. Hodgkin: A Memoir* (London, 1937), pp. 47, 51

From his medical training at St. Thomas's Hospital, Henry went on to an East End Mission Hospital in London, the Mildmay; and there he met a staff-nurse from Northern Ireland called Elizabeth Joy Montgomery. On the morning of April 26th 1903, a week after his 26th birthday, he called her to his office. She put on a clean apron and received an offer of marriage, which she had already decided to accept. Her father, later the Moderator of the Presbyterian General Assembly of Ireland, left his fashionable church to go and work in "Mission Hall" in the Shankhill Road—a name we now associate with the fortress of Protestant Belfast; and it was there in the "Albert Hall," as they called it, that Henry T. Hodgkin and Joy were married on December 9th, 1903, and a formidable and enduring partnership was launched on the world. In May 1904 they offered to go to China. A farewell meeting packed to the doors and requiring an overflow was held in the Town Hall in Darlington in March, 1905. In his farewell address, Henry emphasized that he regarded the time as crucial in Chinese and in Christian history. He quoted the great Baptist missionary Timothy Richard: "The Christian church must convert China in 30 years, or it will be unable to do so in 300 years."

The times were critical also for the little Quaker mission to which Henry and Joy, with their infant son Herbert, made their slow way. It took them from March until May 1905 to reach Szechwan, the most westerly province of China, bordering on

Tibet. There were only 24 of them in the mission, including the new arrivals. Eight years earlier, in 1897 the committee of missionaries had been suspended because of personal difficulties among them which were "most discreditable"; and in 1902 the China Committee in London had been forced to report to the Board that "there is serious friction between our missionaries." Shortly afterward, they decided that "there is no hope of better feeling without the withdrawal of some," and a special deputation was sent to the field to sort them out. In these circumstances it must have seemed to the Board that heaven had answered their prayers in the persons of Henry and Joy Hodgkin. They were young and full of enthusiasm and conviction; her strong personality had Ulster sturdiness, and two leading families involved in the mission quarrels came from her province—the mission had indeed been founded by Ulstermen. Henry was a man of commanding authority and already of international prestige. They made a good start, and helped to draw together not merely the little Quaker band, but the wider missionary community. However, Henry almost immediately abandoned medical practice for the field of education.

An ambitious scheme was formed to set up a West China Union University, one of 13 planned in China on the model of successful experiments. In 1906 a site was purchased outside the walls of the capital of the province, Chengtu; the first tiny classes began in 1910. Hodgkin's standing in the student movement and in the academic world, the confidence he inspired in John R. Mott and other American leaders, and his power of cutting through to the meat of decisions, enabled him to help draw into the scheme not merely American and Canadian mission boards, but even the hesitant Anglican "Church Missionary Society." Medieval Cambridge, after all, had grown up in similar circumstances, with colleges begun as halls of residence for poor students, under religious inspiration and control. As there, so here, Hodgkin pleaded that the colleges should have a federal rather than an organic relation to the University. Though he accepted that it was in origin a foreign body, he insisted that the University must have a Chinese name and a plan for ultimate devolution to Chinese control. Besides the planning of the University itself, he faced the difficulty of finding students qualified to enter it. In 1906 he succeeded in setting up an Educational Union for West China, with a full-time secretary and a common curriculum, grading, and system of examinations. In 1908 he himself became secretary of the "West China Conference" of the Anglo-Saxon mission bodies; and by 1913 (after he left) it had got far enough to draw up a "tentative Constitution" for a "United Protestant Church for West China." Ecumenical zeal seemed in sight of rich results.

But these and other successes in which Henry Hodgkin played a key part had to be set against serious difficulties from within and without. The most fundamental and damaging was unexpected, though it might have been foreseen: at school he was bottom in languages. Henry could not learn Chinese; he was tone deaf. He, who had done everything so easily and steadily, had come up against something quite outside his powers. He was limited to work with an interpreter, or with persons able to understand English. He was debarred not merely from the ability to preach the gospel, and from direct and easy contact with individuals, but from that profound knowledge of a people which grows from understanding their thought through their language: "He who has two tongues has two souls."

In addition, he was now—and for the first perceptible time in his life—up against a divided mind. At home, he had easily reconciled his work for the Unions and the Student Movement with his loyalty to the Society of Friends. He had no patience with the argument which we still hear, that we should be Christians first and Quakers second. He wrote later, "from the heart of China," in 1921:

> While understanding the meaning of those who use the phrase, it always seemed to me a particularly unfortunate one, because it threw into opposition two things that were fundamentally one. I am a Quaker because I am a Christian, and it is the devotion I feel towards Christ my Lord that makes me a keen Quaker—neither more or less. That does not imply any doubt that many a man is a Christian who is not a Quaker (and may be a much better one than I), for God fulfils himself in many ways. But it prevents me from entering sympathetically into the attitude of mind that makes an antithesis where there is, to my mind, none.

But in China it turned out not to be so simple. John R. Mott used all his powerful weight and eloquence to persuade Hodgkin to make the YMCA his life's work, the YMCA, rather than a local denominational mission in remote Szechwan. Mott even went to London and twice harangued the FFMA Board on the subject, arguing that the YMCA would win the all-important Chinese students, the future leaders of their country; and that Henry T. Hodgkin was, by experience and temperament, the perfect person to run the YMCA. Henry was keen to accept, but the Board, headed by its chairman, Henry's father, and the secretary, William Wilson, took the view that Henry should first acquire experience in a local situation, before he tried to cope with a national one. The final decision was left to Henry, and he acquiesced regretfully in the view of his father and friends; but from this time forth he was again and again presented with a choice between irreconcilable duties, and when he returned to China after the first World War, he made the opposite decision: he left Szechwan to become secretary of the National Christian Council of China.

The choice between good and evil he seemed to find easy; the choice between good and good impossible. All his life, even up to the final choice of Pendle Hill the tension continued, as he crossed the ocean again and again in the slow sea voyage of those days. There is no personal dilemma so bleak as that of being indispensable in too many places.

In 1910 the general secretary of the FFMA, Dr. William

Wilson, died suddenly on returning from a visit to India; and Henry Hodgkin was brought home from China to take his place, just after his 33rd birthday. He was an effective organizer and an impressive figure, and before he resigned he had carried the Association, in origin an independent body, into full joint recognition by the Yearly Meetings of London and Dublin. But the work was restricted by the outbreak of war in 1914; and the war brought a new turn in Henry Hodgkin's preoccupations. In the spring of 1914, before the war began, he had been the moving spirit in convening a new conference "to focus the thought of the Society." It was to be held in September at Llandudno in North Wales, under the auspices of the Home and Foreign Mission bodies, the Woodbrooke Extension Committee, and Young Friends. It was thus, in origin, purely Quaker; but Henry was clear that the Society needed wider horizons, and he empanneled speakers from other denominations: the Anglican rector of Rusholme in Manchester; a Presbyterian minister from London, the Rev. Richard Roberts; a liberal theologian, James Hope Moulton; and a woman social worker noted for her work with down-and-outs, Mrs. Mary Higgs (later, but not then, a Friend). It was an unexpected and astonishing list for a Quaker Conference in 1914.

However, when the Conference convened, the war had started; the program was scrapped, and discussion centered on the war and the issues arising from it. Some argued for "defensive war" and justified the Allies' defense of "little Belgium"; others took the pacifist line that Christians could have no part in any war. Hodgkin had hitherto shown little interest in peace debates or the newly fashionable "social gospel," though he sympathized with the women's movement and the labor movement. In this as in other matters he refused to be doctrinaire or to criticize the government of the day; he even denied that he was against the use of *all* force. "I am not myself sure as to the principle of the sanctity of human life, as it is held by man," he wrote in a subsequent controversy with Principal Cairns. His religion had always been Christocentric, his interests lay in evangelization; and it is fascinating to watch the evolution of the new, pacifist, socially oriented Hodgkin. When Pendle Hill finally got its definition, it was "A Quaker Center for Social and Religious Study"—it was Howard Brinton later, and not Henry T. Hodgkin, who altered the title to give religion the priority.

Henry was in part affected by the sessions at the Llandudno Conference, where the argument was of high quality, and where Richard Roberts, the Presbyterian minister from London, who had also not started out as a pacifist, made a profound impression on all who heard him—and in part by experiences a month earlier. On July 31st, five days before the declaration of war, the Hodgkins had reached Constance in Switzerland to attend the inaugural meeting of a new ecumenical body, "The World Alliance for Promoting International Friendship through the Churches." The Hodgkins' best friends at Constance were the Kaiser's chaplain, Dr. F. Siegmund-Schültze, and his wife. When the meeting broke up the German Emperor guaranteed their safety, and the Schultzes shepherded them on their way. They parted with a resolve that their friendship should not be broken, and that they would work for peace. "Remember no matter what happens, it will always be the same between us," said Henry Hodgkin. Around them the desolation of war was already evident; "The sound that remains in our ears was the sobbing of women," one of their party wrote. The pulpits were already resounding with mutual hate. Impatient with the treachery of the churches, and seeking the roots of war in the social order, Henry T. Hodgkin became a pacifist and a socialist.

After the Llandudno Conference, some of those who had participated continued to meet in London at the house of Richard Roberts, in the hope that pacifists and non-pacifists might find a way to bear a common witness as Christians in the war situation. They drew in, among others, prominent Anglicans like William Temple (the future Archbishop of Canterbury), G. K. A. Bell (future Bishop of Chichester) and Percy Dearmer; and Free Churchmen like Fearon Halliday, W. E. Orchard, Maude Royden and Lilian Stevenson. With Temple as editor, they published a series of 48 papers under the general title of *Papers for Wartime;* and they appealed to the Archbishop of Canterbury to convene at Lambeth Palace a conference on the church's duty and function. But the points of view proved irreconcilable; a paper written by Henry Hodgkin for the series was refused by the editorial committee, and the pacifists withdrew to form their own independent organization. They met in Cambridge in the last days of 1914 with the help of Dr. Bell, then chaplain of Trinity Hall, one of the colleges there, and agreed to found a new interdenominational pacifist body, *The Fellowship of Reconciliation*. It held its first conference in the summer of 1915. It had a Quaker chairman—Hodgkin of course—and a Quaker secretary, Lucy Gardner, later a leading figure in the "Faith and Order Movement" of the twenties. In the spring of 1915, when America was still neutral, Hodgkin came to America to promote—guardedly—an American F.O.R.: "It is not for me, an Englishman, to start such a movement in America," he said. But at a gathering which he convened at Garden City, Long Island it happened. In November 1915 he wrote to Joy:

> Just now the pull of America is very strong on me, and I wonder whether some day I shan't want to bring thee and the children over here for a year or two, and try to make a more serious contribution to the problems than I have yet been able to make. Every visit to America seems to leave me more work here in prospect. America is so big and has such big problems and is so hopeful and yet so full of possibilities of evil that I can't resist its call.

There would be other visits. In the summer of 1922 Hodgkin spoke about the F. O. R. at Woolman School, the precursor of Pendle Hill. But it would be 15 years before the intention expressed in his letter was carried out. In 1915 he was still secretary of the Friends Foreign Mission Association. When he was one of the handful of people given unconditional exemption from military service, he was bound to demonstrate his faith by constant speaking at public meetings, often in personal danger; by visiting prisons and working for conscientious objectors there; by enduring the obloquy of old friends, and by working for war relief and for civil liberties on endless committees. At the end of the war he was chairman of the Jerusalem and Palestine Relief Fund. He took part in the efforts of the Scandinavian bishops headed by Archbishop Soderblom of Uppsala, to call an International Christian Conference to mediate in the war. And after hostilities ceased he and Joy went on a Scandinavian tour to pick up Quaker and pacifist contacts and promote action for peace. For the Fellowship of Reconciliation he wrote two volumes, *A Lay Religion* and *The Christian Revolution*.

Once more the call of China prevailed; a special edition of *The Christian Revolution* with local illustrations was prepared, and Henry travelled the country to persuade the Chinese that the revolution they needed was a loving, non-violent one. By January 1922 he had delivered (in English, of course) 420 lectures and addresses expounding his ideas in Shanghai, Peking, Canton, Hong Kong, Nanking, Hankow, Mukden, Wuchang, and many other places. His hopes were still ecumenical, though his strictures on the existing churches were severe. A few quotations from *A Lay Religion* will show how literally he interpreted its title:

> Jesus Christ drove "the religious specialist" right off the field. The specialist was there in force. Looked at through the stinging epithets of Jesus, he seems to us a particularly disagreeable animal. But he is with us today as arrogant as ever, as ready to bind burdens on others which he is unwilling to lift with his little finger. Jesus saw the outcast and the harlot entering the Kingdom of Heaven before the "religious specialist". Today we assume that the spectral progeny of these specialists will get there first.

> The champion of the common man is needed again today to shiver this tyranny with the shaft of simple, unadulterated truth.
>
> *Lay Religions*, p. 42

The "religious specialists" he defined as the priest, the theologian and the "saint"—that is, of course, the pretended saint, not the real one. "It is a matter of common knowledge," he claimed, "that

> the ordinary presentation of religion is not *real*. It is surrounded with subterfuge and sham; it is associated with medieval ceremonies; it is couched in language that is out of date and meaningless to any who have not been brought up to drink it in; it is careful to run away from things that really matter. The "religious" man lives in a world of his own making, and it seems to the common man an unreal world,—a world of shams.
>
> Ibid., p. 53

This came, he thought, from the hypocrisy of having to pretend, in conduct and especially in "the bondage of preaching" . . . "an unspeakable and bitter bondage . . . from which it seems impossible to escape":

> The truth is uttered glibly, and without any clear conception of what it would imply if it were really put into action. Or it is withheld in whole or in part, lest it should offend the wealthy and influential members of the congregation. Or it is fenced round with all the arguments of expediency so that it may hurt no man's feelings . . .
>
> Ibid., p. 51

The "representative of religion" is compelled to disguise his own "sins of pride and temper, jealousy and self-seeking" by the "compulsion to set forth only the highest ideals—to do less seems to be disloyal to Christ."

Strong stuff. Yet Henry Hodgkin returned to China, still dreaming that the churches might be redeemed. Concerning what Christian unity might mean, he had a very different view from that of the doctrinal debates, that droned on interminably, then as now:

> Jesus Christ called his followers into a piece of work so utterly

beyond their powers, so much too big for isolated efforts, so hazardous and so glorious, that they were welded, in the white heat of a great endeavor into a deep unity. When this happens again, there will be little, if any, need to have ecclesiastics and theologians devoting their best efforts to problems of church unity. It will have come not by tinkering compromises, by formulae that hide differences or by mechanical repetition of creeds and observance of rites, but by the sheer necessity of the case. Those who are truly possessed by the spirit of Jesus must find themselves bound into one body, whatever their name or sign, as they really face these problems.

Ibid., p. 105

After four years' preparation, a Conference was convened in Shanghai in May 1922 by representatives of all the 130 Protestant denominations working in 18 provinces of China. A Chinese Christian, Dr. Cheng Ching-yi, presided. It formed a National Christian Council of China, and invited Hodgkin to become joint secretary. He accepted, and he worked in China until he came to Pendle Hill. Henry described his dream in glowing terms, as

> a task of surprising magnitude and splendour . . . the working out of all the implications of Christs's way . . . under the inspiration of the new churches of the Orient, using the stores of their ancient philosophies and ethics.

From this, one would imagine that his decision was final and wholehearted; yet it was not—his heart was still divided. At the end of his first term of office in China, on leave in England in 1924, Henry received from the Fellowship of Reconciliation an urgent appeal to become its British secretary. He had a young family and he was conscious that they suffered neglect, as children do in such circumstances. Joy had to stay part of the time in England with them, and longed for a settled home. He wrote to his father:

> There are times when I itch to be at the job in England and Europe, where the danger points seem to lie. This F.O.R. call comes at a moment and in a way that certainly makes a special appeal. I do not now feel able to reach a decision . . .

He thought of his "insufficient Chinese" and of the discouragements he had suffered; but in the end he went back to China.

These discouragements had begun in Szechwan. In the missionary community there he noted "a failure to appreciate the deep significance of the times in which we are living," hours frittered away in controversy over "verbal inspiration" and the Second Coming, and "something very like an inquisition into the faith of individual missionaries. I was quite unprepared for anything as bad as I feel this to be." But at the National Council things were no better. Many of the missions were staffed by Fundamentalists who found their deep but narrow faith to be the source of strength to support them in almost intolerable conditions of civil turmoil, personal discomfort, public indifference and physical danger. They were restive under the attempts of Hodgkin and his friends to change them. He reported trouble over "the over-insistence of the ultra-evangelicals on the inerrant Word of God in all its 64 books;" and at a 1923 Convention in Kuling they found a way to censure their secretary by reducing the number of lectures he was to give from 6 to 3. He deplored the controversy as "simply devilish," and in a severe mood declared that if all the missionaries were withdrawn from China and all funds stopped, the Chinese church would be united in a generation.

In 1926, during his second term of office, there was fission. The Fundamentalist bodies, about one-third of the membership but including the revered China Inland Mission, which had been the god-parent of the Quakers in Szechwan, withdrew from the National Christian Council, taking Dr. Cheng with them. The High-church Episcopalians also withdrew, leaving the National Christian Council religiously incomplete and politically ineffective. It failed even to persuade the reactionary Shanghai Municipal Council (on which no Chinese sat) to abolish, or even to control effectively, the factories in Shanghai where little girls worked all night.

Henry and Joy Hodgkin lived in a beautiful apartment in Shanghai, that focal point of western capitalist Imperialism at its most aggressive (and consequently the birthplace of the Chinese Communist party and of the People's Republic). It was, of course, inevitable that the headquarters of the National Christian Council should be situated there; it was also disastrous. Henry suffered from inner qualms, and by stifling them placed himself in that half-light of hypocrisy which he had so eloquently denounced. These qualms had been in him for a long time. They were already expressed on the long river journey when he left Szechwan in 1921. He wrote on the boat a series of Quakerly queries to himself:

> Is the state of luxury that separates us from even the best of our native fellow workers really necessary?
>
> Ought we to become Chinese subjects and give up our national rights, especially when we are protected by extra-territoriality?
>
> Have we been afraid to speak the truth about our own failure, that of our own churches and countries, and so put back the cause of truth?

"It is the height of folly" he wrote in the same letter to his 500 correspondents at home, "to try and represent Christendom as anywhere near Christian"—so it seems that his answer to the third query was "Yes." Presumably his answer to the first question about the luxurious style of Western living was also "Yes," but a solution lay beyond his powers. What would Joy have done, living in Chinese style, and how would they have survived without even enough linguistic skill to make ordinary contact with their neighbors?

During the last period of their service in China, Henry Hodgkin abandoned hope for the Protestant churches as he knew them, and began to build an alternative vision of the inter-penetration of faiths and cultures, fed by the sympathy he felt for Chinese Buddhism. The infant church in the first centuries, he held, had been created from the fusion of its Jewish inheritance with the philosophy of Greece and the organization of Rome. Now the cultures of India, China and Japan must be fused with the Western inheritance in like manner:

> A great task of rethinking our central ideas opens up before us, and as the Greek and Roman Fathers performed the task in the first three or four centuries of our era, the Chinese and Indian fathers must perform it today.

He dreamed that

> Chinese Christianity might interpret Christianity in a far more thoroughgoing way than anything that is current in the West. It might startle our staid Christianity into a new certainty, a deeper faith, a stronger love, and in a tide of common life and light, who knows how many abuses might be swept away?

At the farewell meeting in Darlington, when he left for China in 1905, Henry Hodgkin had quoted Timothy Richards dictum that the Christian Church must convert China within 30 years. It had failed to do so.

From mass action, Henry Hodgkin turned to the few. He thought the immediate Western contribution must be made through "such intimate relations with the few as will enable them to catch all that is best in our spirits, and to take up the burdens we may have to lay down." But he and Joy were automatically barred from this intimacy by their lack of language and their way of life; and in a recurrent change of mood, Henry was already involved before he left China finally in 1929, with approaches from the group in America who were planning Pendle Hill. The Friends Foreign Mission Association which he had served for fifteen years as missionary and as General Secretary had already disappeared into history; he had helped by his generous support of Carl Heath's fresh ideas to create the new Friends Service Council which London Yearly Meeting inaugurated in 1926. He himself, of course, was not there for its muddled birth, though it would have undoubtedly been better if he had been. He had written asking that preparation should be made by "a time of prayer" (like one of his "retreats"), asking that "for once, at least, let everything be said that can be said"; and preferably "in a meeting composed largely of those under forty on whom responsibility must soon fall, if it has not already fallen," with "all the cards on the table." None of that, of course, happened; and Henry was in search of a place where it could happen. He was looking for the mount of vision—for Pendle Hill. Here he hoped that his belief in the reality of religion and the adventure of its search would prevail. He had written in 1918 in *A Lay Religion:*

> To sum up, men are fundamentally religious. The essentially religious demand is for reality. When unreality invades religion, the very foundations of the life of man are being sapped, or (to change the simile) the wells from which we draw the water of life are poisoned. This is what has happened in our own day. The great need of our time is to shatter the unreality, and bring men back to truth. The way to find the truth is for each of us to examine his own actions, and from them deduce what his actual religion is. From that starting-point and from that alone, can we begin to find our way to that religion by which we ought to live (p. 59).

Pendle Hill was to be a cell provided for that starting point. He brought to it long experience in many fields and at all levels, and the immense prestige which would override doubts and objections. He brought his skill in planning, and realism in assessing the possibilities. He brought sharp criticism of existing education, especially higher education:

> this education has left [youth] uncertain and vague as to the compulsive meanings of life that demand their allegiance . . . there has been strikingly little integration of their lives around any consuming moral, social, or spiritual passion.

The intellect alone was not enough: "Only a vulgar fraction of a man can be produced by intellectual culture." The "fearless pursuit of truth" was essential; "there is no safety in closing our eyes." He sought "a synthesis of religious, scientific and aesthetic thought." Many students, he declared "will find the richest part of Pendle Hill outside the stated courses." He proposed "to use work and play, and especially our periods of joint recreation as a means of deepening our sympathies as well as enlarging our interests." But he also realized that "There is an element of isolation or solitariness in the greatest personalities as well as development through stimulating fellowship"; and he believed that every student should have a separate room, and that eventually the center must have a place of meditation.

He denied that Pendle Hill was "a modern monastery," and wanted "something better than asceticism." He strenuously opposed those who asked for starkness, and thought there could be no better use for beautiful houses and gardens than for a purpose like this. He wanted the work of the house to be, as it still is, "shared by all with a minimum of outside help." There must be "No rules, no credits, no penalities," but "the fellowship of a small group where students and faculty together work at the problems considered and share in their devotional life." It would arise from "the conviction that there are resources in the spiritual world far greater than we commonly use, and the effort to understand their laws and make them available for human progress," using "such practical mysticism as is illustrated in the experience of the Society of Friends," with "the determination to take the religion of Christ seriously, and to think out its relation to every aspect of life."

The history of how, stage by stage, these dreams were implemented lies in Eleanore Mather's forthcoming history, and the debt of Pendle Hill to its predecessor, the Woolman School, has already been described in Carol Murphy's Pendle Hill pamphlet, *The Roots of Pendle Hill.* I propose only to stress the strenuous wholeheartedness with which the Hodgkins committed themselves to the scheme, and the price they paid for it. They were still in China when they received a letter from the interested group in Philadelphia in July 1928, and cabled a reply expressing interest. Early in 1929 they returned to England via Siberia; and by March Henry was on his way to America (by ship, don't forget) to discuss details. It was the first of three trips he made that year—an instance of his indefatigable voyaging. In March, and again in September, he incubated this project as he had done other projects since his student days, in retreats—in this case held at Westtown.

Early practices still endure: Monday night Extension Lectures, to reach a public off-campus; the proviso that "No student shall take more than three courses" (later rephrased to be "two, or at most, three"); and most astonishing of all, considering the short span of attention which is now accepted, and the general practice in other places, a call for classes which should last from two to two and a half hours, and which must involve, as they still do, the "interplay of student and teacher." But we find this combined endearingly with Henry's own incisive streak:

> I think the deep interest of each one must be secured, while we, of course, must have our own distinct ideas as to what we want to give the students.

He asked for "perfect frankness and sincerity," and hoped to develop "the kind of criticism which grows and deepens friendship, in place of that which breaks up and embitters"; and he hoped that, in the domestic context, there might be a growth of confidence and "mutual understanding between members of different Quaker groups" to which he, as an outsider, might make a personal contribution: "It is our function to help in the discovery and strengthening of the deeper unities without which no plan can amount to much."

Most of the big things that Henry T. Hodgkin served have gone into oblivion together with the world he lived in—the whole Foreign Mission movement, the Friends Foreign Mission Association, the Szechwan group, the National Christian Council of China, the committees he chaired, the Boards for which he raised money. The Christian Revolution for which he hoped has still to take place. But the seed was planted, and grows.

Publications by Henry T. Hodgkin
Chronologically arranged
(This list does not claim to be complete)

STUDIES IN THE EPISTLE TO THE HEBREWS. Written for the Student Christian Movement Bible Study Groups. London, 1902.

THE MESSAGE AND MISSION OF QUAKERISM, with William Charles Braithwaite. Published by direction of the Five Years Meeting. Philadelphia: John C. Winston Co., 1912.

"The Church's Opportunity in the Present Crisis." Written for the series, PAPERS FOR WARTIME, but rejected by the editorial committee, London, 1914.

THE WAY OF THE GOOD PHYSICIAN. London: United Council on Missionary Education, 1915.

FRIENDS BEYOND THE SEAS. Written for the Jubilee of the Friends Foreign Mission Ass'n of London and Dublin. London, 1916.

THE MISSIONARY MOTIVE AND THE PRESENT OPPORTUNITY. The Swarthmore Lecture of London Yearly Meeting. London, 1916.

LAY RELIGION. Written for the series, THE CHRISTIAN REVOLUTION. London: Headley Brothers, 1918.

THE CHRISTIAN REVOLUTION. In the same series, but developed from a prize-winning essay submitted to the Walker Trustees of the University of St. Andrews, Scotland, in 1919, on the theme of "Spiritual Regeneration as the Basis of World Reconstruction." London: Swarthmore Press, 1921 (Shanghai ed. 1922).

CHINA IN THE FAMILY OF NATIONS. Lectures given at Selly Oak, Birmingham, Eng. New York: George H. Doran Co., 1923.

THE WAY OF JESUS. Bible study book for use in China. New York: George H. Doran Co., 1923.

JESUS AMONG MEN. Bible study book for use in China. New York: Richard R. Smith, Inc., 1930.

LIVING ISSUES IN CHINA. New York: Friendship Press, 1932.

SEEING OURSELVES THROUGH RUSSIA, ed. Henry T. Hodgkin, based on work of first year's class in social problems at Pendle Hill. New York: Ray Long and Richard R. Smith, Inc., 1932.